MAKE IT!

Fashion Design

Leigh Anne Balzekas &
Kristine Ownley

Rourke
Educational Media

rourkeeducationalmedia.com

SUPPLIES TO COMPLETE ALL PROJECTS:

- 1 to 2 yards (0.91 to 1.83 meters) of elastic
- 2 to 6 yards (1.83 to 5.5 meters) of fabric, old sheets, or curtains
- 3 to 4 yards (2.74 to 3.66 meters) grosgrain ribbon
- circle skirt pattern
- clear tape
- clips, clothespins, or rubber bands
- fabric scissors
- fabric to dye (t-shirt, cloth bag, etc.)
- flexible measuring tape
- iron
- large paper, or smaller pages taped together
- pen
- pencil
- pins with plastic heads
- push pins
- rubber gloves
- salt

- scissors for paper (don't use your fabric scissors!)
- sewing machine
- tailor's chalk
- thread
- wooden blocks (optional)

Table of Contents

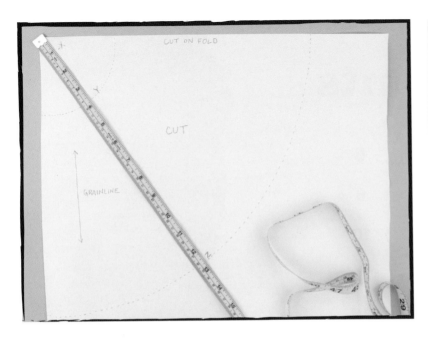

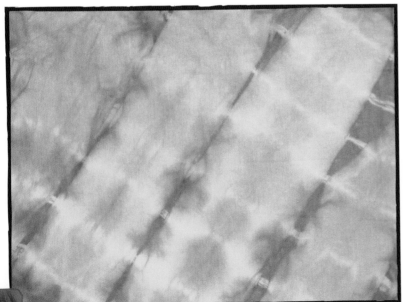

Get Started in Fashion Design

Sourcing is the process of determining how and where your materials will be obtained. Sourcing your fabrics can help you learn how clothes are constructed.

Enter the world of fashion design by starting with the basics. Soon you'll be creating clothes for you, your friends, and your family!

Pattern Making: Circle Skirt

CUT ON FOLD

YOU WILL NEED:

- flexible measuring tape
- large paper, or smaller pages taped together
- clear tape
- scissors for paper (don't use your fabric scissors!)
- pen/pencil
- push pin

CUT

GRAINLINE

Tip:
It's easier to do this where you can spread out. Try a large table or the floor.

MAKE YOUR PATTERN!

Learn how to flat pattern a basic circle skirt. This pattern can be turned into a wrap skirt or an apron.

Here's How:

1. Measure your waist with a flexible measuring tape.

2. Add a seam allowance of 1 inch (2.54 centimeters) for each seam. This skirt has two seams. Two seams = 2 inches (5.08 centimeters).

3. For an elastic waist, add 2 inches (5.08 centimeters).

4. Decide how much **volume** or fullness you want in the skirt. The full circle will use the most fabric, have the most movement, and the most volume. The quarter circle will use the least fabric, have less movement, and the least volume.

5. Multiply your final measurement by the fractions below for the radius measurement.
Full Circle = 0.167
Three Quarter Circle = 0.2
Half Circle = 0.314
Quarter Circle = 0.667
This measurement is your radius, shown as x to y on the pattern.

6. Measure how long you want the skirt to be. Then add your seam allowance for the hem and waist, a total of 2 inches (5.08 centimeters). Example: 25 inches + 2 inches = 27 inches (63.5 centimeters + 5.08 centimeters = 68.58 centimeters). This measurement is your length, shown as y to z on the pattern.

Create Your Pattern

7. Place the end of the measuring tape at the corner of the paper. Hold in place with a push pin. Move the measuring tape from one side of the paper to the other, marking where y and z hit the paper at all points.

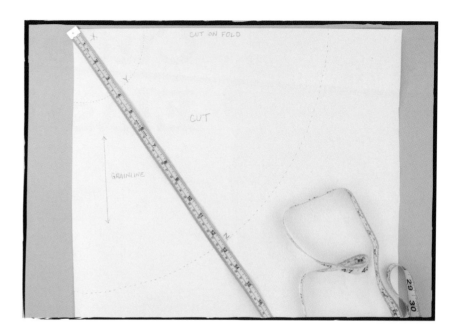

8. Connect the dots on the paper, and cut out the pattern. Write the instructions "cut on fold" and "cut 2" onto the pattern. This will remind you how to fold the fabric and how many of these you need to make the skirt.

9. Now you have a completed pattern that you can use again and again!

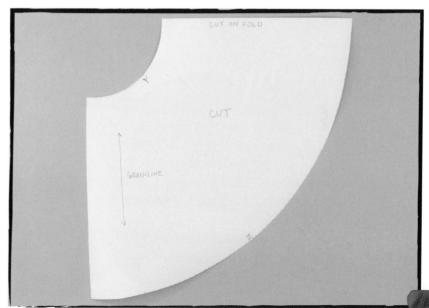

Cut and Sew: Elastic-Waist Skirt

YOU WILL NEED:

- 2 to 3 yards (1.83 to 2.74 meters) of fabric, old sheets, or curtains
- 1 to 2 yards (0.91 to 1.83 meters) of elastic

- circle skirt pattern
- flexible measuring tape
- fabric scissors
- pins with plastic heads
- sewing machine
- tailor's chalk
- thread

Tip:
Fabric scissors are just scissors that never cut anything but fabric. If you use them on paper, they become dull. This makes it difficult to cut a clean line on fabric. Mark your fabric scissors so you don't get them mixed up!

MAKE YOUR SKIRT!

Here's How:

1. Find the **selvage** edge of your fabric. The selvage is the raw edge. If you're using sheets, it's one of the straight edges.

2. Depending on the type of circle skirt you chose in project one, you will fold the fabric one of two ways: Selvage edges together, where the fold is parallel to the selvage edge, or cut edges together, where the fold is **perpendicular** to the selvage edge. Hold up your pattern to make sure it fits on the fabric.

Tip: If you have a large piece of fabric, and you are using the second folding technique, you can fold the cut edges into the middle to save fabric.

FABRIC FOLDING DIAGRAM

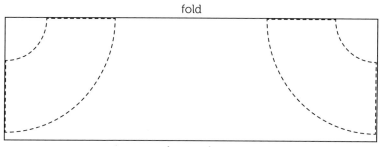

Selvage edge to selvage edge

fold

selvage edge

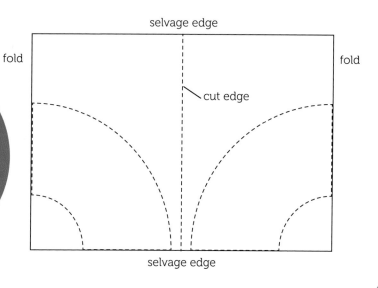

Fold the cut edge into the center

selvage edge

fold · fold

cut edge

selvage edge

3. Lay the paper pattern over the folded fabric. Use heavy objects such as books or rocks to hold the fabric down.

4. Cut the fabric around the pattern.

5. Repeat steps 2 through 4 for the second skirt piece.

Tip:

This is where the directions "cut on fold" come in. Make sure that it is lined up with where you folded the fabric.

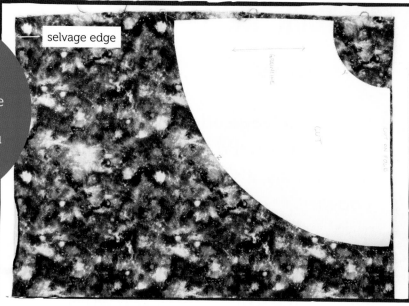

selvage edge

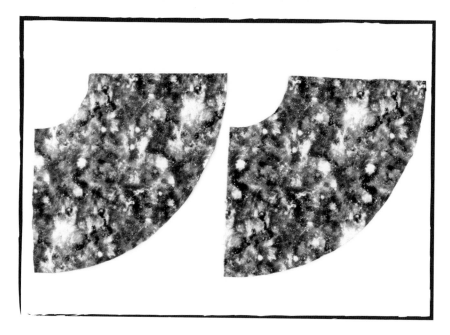

Sew:

1. Sew a basting stitch along the waist to prevent the fabric from stretching. A basting stitch is a temporary straight stitch that holds layers together until a final stitch is sewn.

2. Locate the side seams.

3. Line up the side seams from the first piece and the second piece. Pin them with the right sides of the fabric together.

Tip: When pinning a seam, place the pins with the heads facing away from the seam. This way they're easier to remove when sewing!

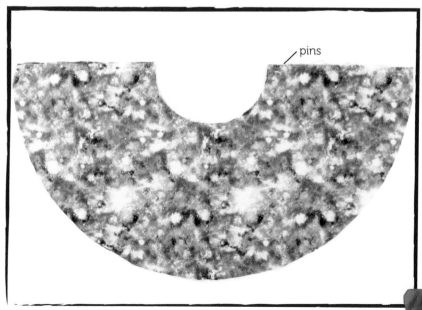

pins

4. Starting at the top or bottom, sew together both side seams, using a half inch (1.27 centimeter) seam allowance. Be sure to back stitch to secure the beginning and ending of the seam.

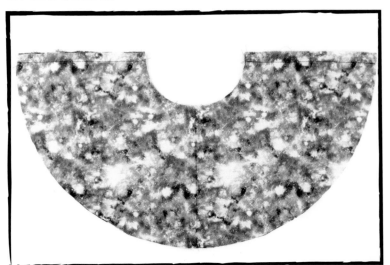 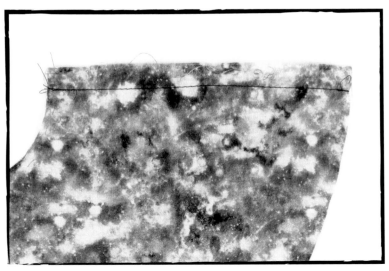

5. Find the center of the front and the back and place a pin on both.

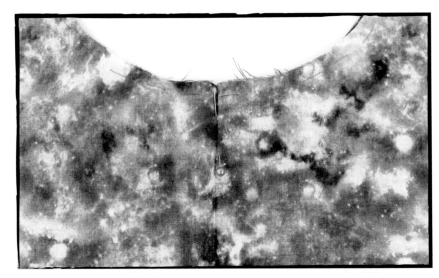

6. Place the elastic around the waist of the person who will wear the skirt. Hold the elastic tight and make sure it's comfortable. Mark with tailor's chalk.

7. Use a zig zag stitch to sew the elastic where it's marked by placing one side over the other flat.

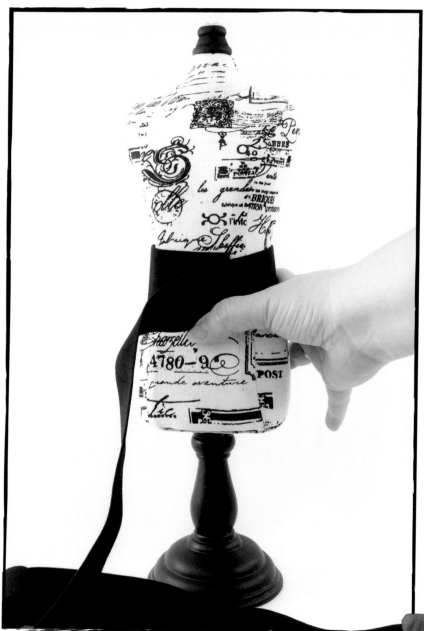

8. Divide the waistband into quadrants, marking with pins.

9. Place the waistband over the top edge of the skirt and match up pins at the side seams, front and back. The back will be the sewn seam of the elastic.

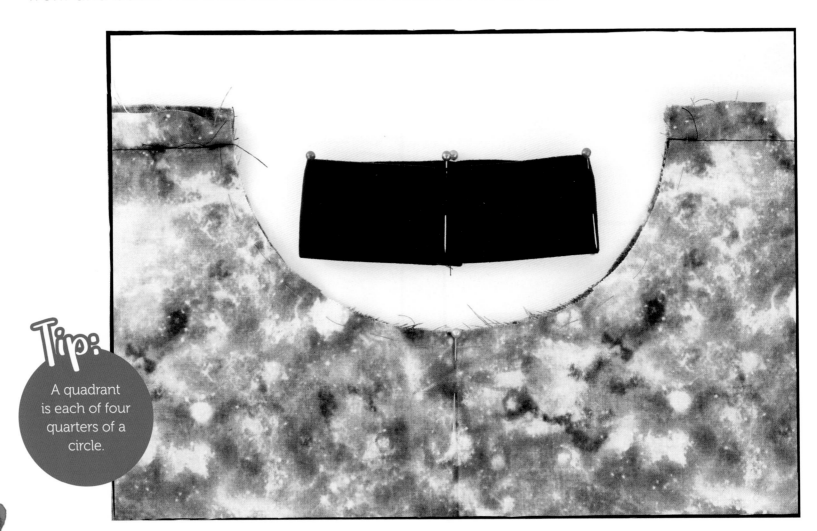

Tip:
A quadrant is each of four quarters of a circle.

10. Your skirt will be bigger than your elastic. Going by quadrant, work your way around the waist, pinning the skirt into the waistband by folding it little by little. Marking the quadrants will help you make sure the fullness of the skirt is evenly distributed.

11. Using a zig zag stitch, sew the skirt to the elastic waistband.

Tip: Sew with the right side facing up to make sure your stitch looks pleasing from the outside. Your pins will help you keep the skirt in place as you sew.

12. Zig zag stitch the hem edge to finish. Press up the hem allowance, and sew the hem in place with a straight stitch.

Tip:
There are many kinds of hems and seam finishes. Explore different techniques as you learn.

Pressing

Pressing means using the iron to press down on the seam or hem. Hold, then bring the iron up and back down on the next section. You don't want to pull the iron along the seam during the construction process because this tension could stretch the fabric, causing puckering and distortion. Adding heat seals the seam by slightly fusing the new thread into the fabric. This will make the seams stronger and sturdier. Pressing also smooths out your hems and seams so they look crisp.

Design and Sew: Wrap Skirt

YOU WILL NEED:

- 1 to 3 yards (0.91 to 2.74 meters) of fabric, old sheets, or curtains
- 3 to 4 yards (2.74 to 3.66 meters) grosgrain ribbon
- sewing machine
- iron
- thread
- fabric scissors
- pencil
- pins with plastic heads
- circle skirt pattern

MAKE A WRAP SKIRT!

Here's How:

1. Fold your fabric selvage to selvage. If you're using several pieces of fabric, each piece must be lined up on the same **grainline**.

2. If you're making an apron, cut out one of the circle skirt pieces (one on the fold, or two not on the fold). If you are making a wrap skirt, cut out one extra circle skirt panel (three on the fold, or six not on the fold).

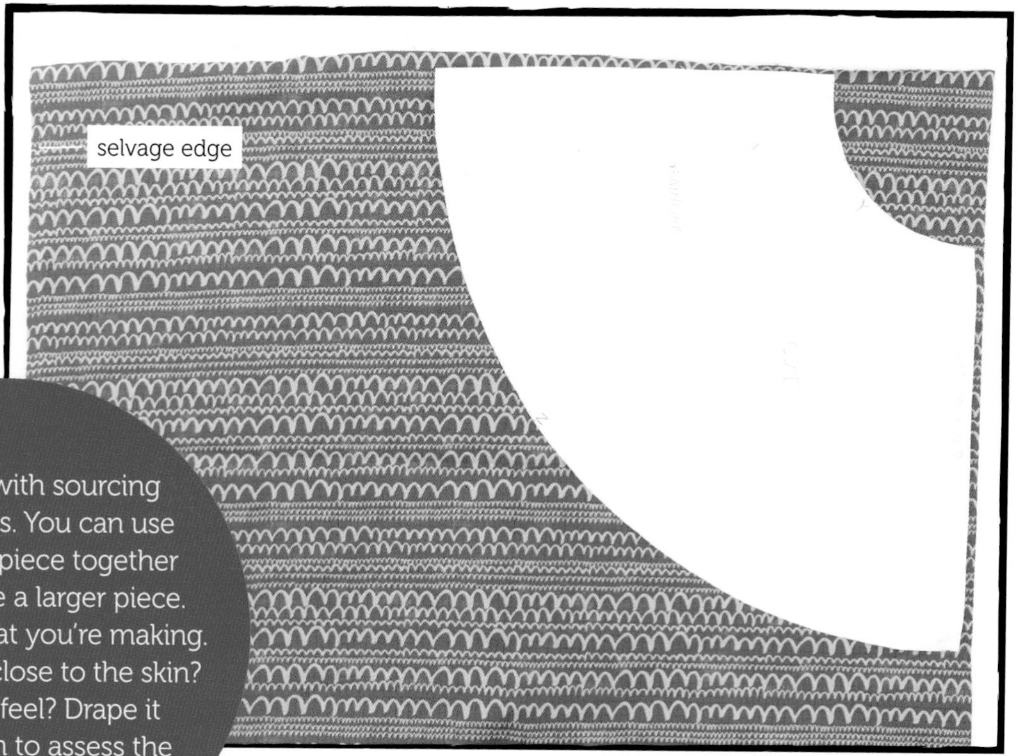

selvage edge

Tip:
Be creative with sourcing your materials. You can use one fabric, or piece together scraps to make a larger piece. Think about what you're making. Will it be worn close to the skin? How does it feel? Drape it over your arm to assess the movement and stretch.

3. For a wrap skirt, assemble your panels by sewing side seams together just like you did with the elastic waist skirt, pinning and straight stitching. Make sure you leave the last seam open. For an apron, just hem the edges.

4. Press seams down.

5. Hem the bottom the same way you hemmed the elastic waist skirt. You can also try a new technique.

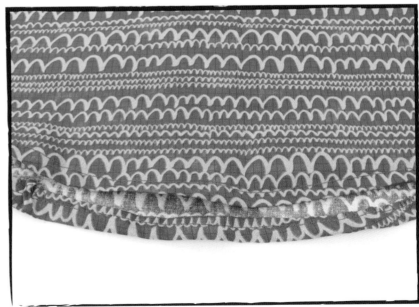

6. Find the middle of your skirt or apron by folding it in half. Mark with a pin. Do the same for the ribbon.

7. Place the ribbon, matching the marked pins together, and pin the length of the skirt/apron along the ribbon a half inch (1.27 centimeters) from the edge.

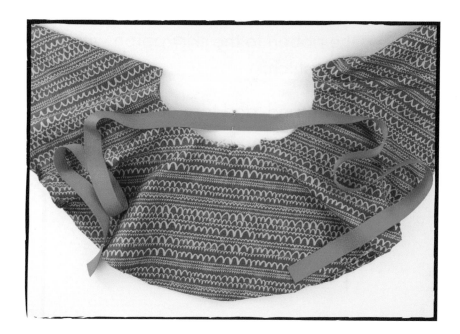

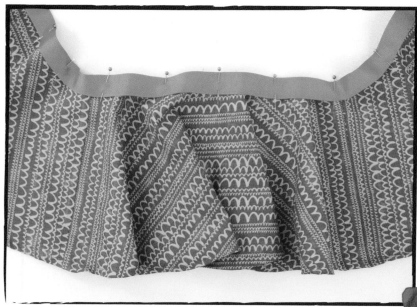

8. Sew the ribbon to the skirt/apron with a zig zag stitch.

9. Wrap it around, and trim ribbon to desired length.

Fabric Manipulation: Shibori Dyeing

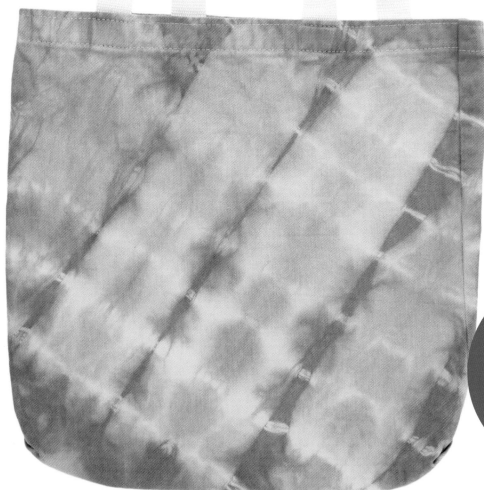

YOU WILL NEED:

- fabric
- dye
- rubber gloves
- clips, clothespins, or rubber bands
- wooden blocks (optional)
- salt

Tip:

There are many ways to create your own patterns. Experiment with different found objects to create unique designs!

Shibori is an ancient Japanese dyeing technique that uses binding and folding to create a pattern. Where the fabric is bound, it will stay the original color. The rest will be dyed. The more color you want, the less you should bind it. There are several ways to Shibori dye:

Kumo – This method uses fabric wrapped over marbles or stones secured with rubber bands.

Nui – This method also uses bunched fabric, but the binding is created through stitching with thread.

Kanoko – The fabric is rolled or folded into a long rod shape, and bound with rubber bands, or tied with string, to create the pattern.

Itajime – The fabric is accordion-folded and pressed between wooden blocks and bound with rubber bands.

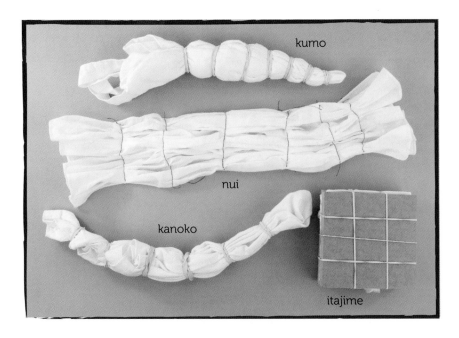

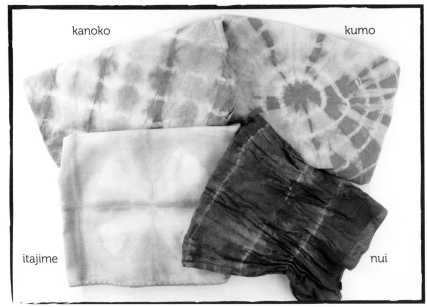

26

MAKE A SHIBORI DYED TOTE!

Here's How:

1. Wash fabric to be dyed.

2. Choose how you want to fold or roll the fabric. How do you want the fabric to look? An accordion fold, square fold, or triangle fold will produce a more geometric, repeated pattern. Bunching or rolling the fabric will produce a pattern with more movement and variety.

3. Attach clips, clothespins, or rubber bands to folded fabric. Where you place the clips will remain the base color, and what is left will become dyed.

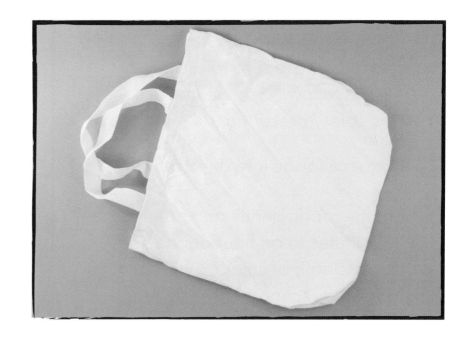

Tip:

If you are using blocks, place the blocks on either side of the folded fabric, and bind with rubber bands or twine. If you rolled or bunched your fabric, wrap the rolled or bunched fabric with rubber bands or twine. The tighter you wrap it, the more the original color will show through.

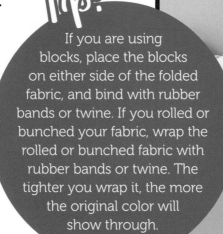

4. Prepare **dye bath** with hot water, salt, and dye. Make sure to use gloves. Always follow package instructions and safety precautions.

5. Immerse fabric into dye bath.

6. Stir the fabric gently and often for 30 minutes to an hour depending on the depth of color desired and the dye directions.

Tip:

Cover your work area so the dye doesn't stain anything it's not supposed to!

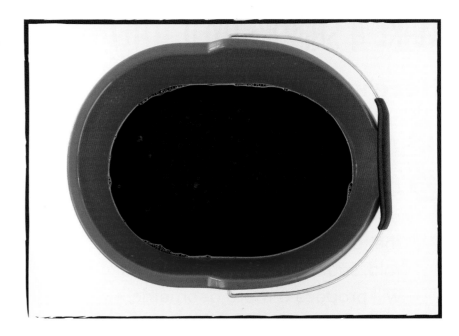

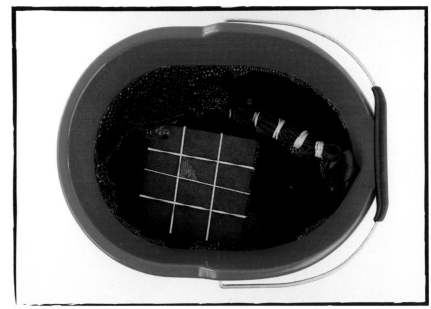

7. Remove the fabric and rinse with cool water until the water runs clear.

8. Wash the fabric with gentle detergent and dry.

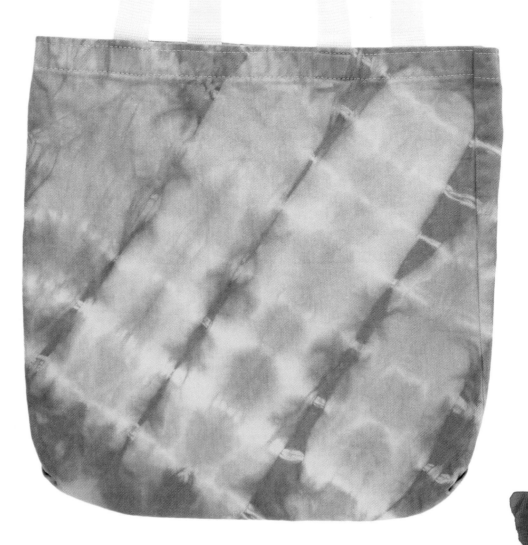

Glossary

dye bath (die BATH): the combination of dye, water, and salt that fabric is immersed into color

grainline (GRAIN-line): the woven thread that makes up the fabric that runs parallel or perpendicular to the selvage edge

perpendicular (pur-puhn-DIK-yuh-lur): straight up and down

selvage (SELL-vage): an edge produced on woven fabric during manufacturing that prevents it from unraveling

volume (VAHL-yuhm): the amount of space taken up by an object

Index

Show What You Know

1. How do you fold fabric before you line up and cut out your pattern?

2. When dyeing fabric, what effect does binding create?

3. What is the difference between nui and kumo dyeing methods?

4. What other things can you make from a circle skirt pattern?

5. How is math used in fashion design?

Further Reading

Plumley, Amie Petronis and Lisle, Andria, *Sewing School: 21 Sewing Projects Kids Will Love to Make*, Storey Publishing, 2010.

Plumley, Amie Petronis and Lisle, Andria, *Sewing School 2: Lessons in Machine Sewing; 20 Projects Kids Will Love to Make*, Storey Publishing, 2013.

Reader's Digest Complete Guide to Sewing, Reader's Digest, 1997.

About the Authors

Leigh Anne Balzekas is a full-time fashion designer and boutique owner. She creates custom wedding dresses and other clothes for her clients. Kristine Ownley is a hairdresser and works with Leigh Anne dyeing custom fabrics for their clothing line, The Disco Dolls Designs.

Meet The Author!
www.meetREMauthors.com

www.rourkeeducationalmedia.com

PHOTO CREDITS: Cover & all pages: © creativelytara

Edited by: Keli Sipperley
Cover and Interior design by: Tara Raymo • CreativelyTara • www.creativelytara.com

Library of Congress PCN Data

Fashion Design / Leigh Anne Balzekas & Kristine Ownley
(Make It!)
ISBN 978-1-64156-441-0 (hard cover)
ISBN 978-1-64156-567-7 (soft cover)
ISBN 978-1-64156-686-5 (e-Book)
Library of Congress Control Number: 2018930469

Rourke Educational Media
Printed in the United States of America,
North Mankato, Minnesota